What Do You
Know about
Maps?

Using

Topographic Maps

Tracy Nelson Maurer

Lerner Publications • Minneapolis

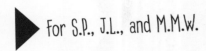

For S.P., J.L., and M.M.W.

Lerner Publications Company
A division of Lerner Publishing Group, Inc.
241 First Avenue North
Minneapolis, MN 55401 USA

For reading levels and more information, look up this title at www.lernerbooks.com.

Library of Congress Cataloging-in-Publication Data

Names: Maurer, Tracy, 1965– author.
Title: Using topographic maps / by Tracy Nelson Maurer.
Description: Minneapolis : Lerner Publications, 2016. | Series: Searchlight books. What do you know about maps? | Includes bibliographical references and index.
Identifiers: LCCN 2015041874| ISBN 9781512409482 (lb : alk. paper) | ISBN 9781512412963 (pb : alk. paper)
Subjects: LCSH: Map reading—Juvenile literature. | Topographic maps—Juvenile literature.
Classification: LCC GA130 .M445 2016 | DDC 912.01/4—dc23

LC record available at http://lccn.loc.gov/2015041874

Manufactured in the United States of America
1-39537-21241-3/14/2016

Contents

Chapter 1

WHAT IS A TOPOGRAPHIC MAP?

Maps combine information from science and math with a touch of art. They represent places and the living and nonliving things there. What each map shows depends on its purpose. Some maps guide travelers. Others show borders between cities or countries. Topographic maps use lines to show the shape and height of Earth's surface.

Lines are a main feature of topographic maps. What do these maps show?

Many maps show only the length or width of a place. A road map, for instance, might show how long a main road is between Denver, Colorado, and Orlando, Florida. Topographic maps are different, since they can show height. They can show that Denver has a higher elevation than Orlando does.

A place's elevation is its height above sea level. Denver (ABOVE) has a high elevation.

How do topographic maps show height? The lines on these maps are called contour lines. They show height by connecting points that are the same elevation. This means that if you trace a single contour line with your finger, all the places along that line will be the same height. Every fifth contour line is usually labeled with the height of the places along that line. You can estimate the elevations of the places along lines without labels too. Just look at how much space is between the lines. If the lines are close together, they mark a steep elevation. If they are far apart, they mark flatter land.

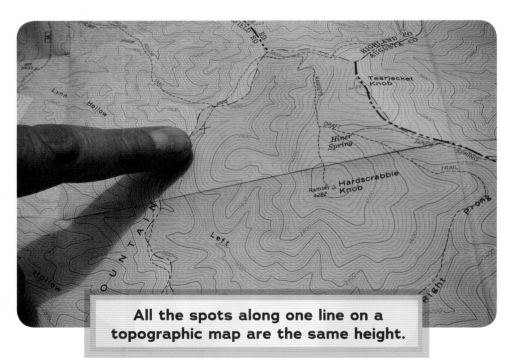

All the spots along one line on a topographic map are the same height.

The History of Topographic Maps

European explorers used the first topographic maps in the seventeenth century. These early maps mostly showed coasts. People in France produced the first full set of topographic maps for any country. They took about a century to make.

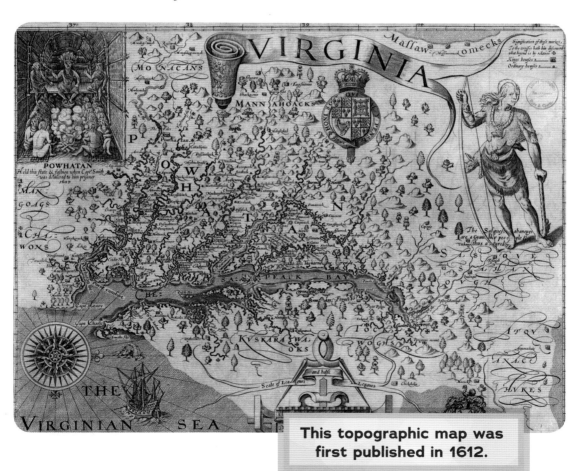

This topographic map was first published in 1612.

Modern Topographic Maps

These days, cartographers, or mapmakers, can make topographic maps much more quickly than past cartographers could. The United States Geological Survey (USGS) creates most of the topographic maps in the United States. They use technology and modern tools to make the maps, including aerial photography; pictures from satellites; and information from GPS, or the global positioning system.

Modern cartographers have many more tools to help them than past cartographers did.

The Thrill of Mapmaking

Surveyors measure and examine land to gather information cartographers can use to make maps. In the past, surveying work was very dangerous. Diseases, frostbite, and falls killed many surveyors. But surveying expeditions were also exciting! Sir George Everest spent twenty-five years mapping India. The world's tallest mountain, Mount Everest in Tibet, is named after him.

Mount Everest is 29,035 feet (8,850 meters) high!

Chapter 2

WHAT'S ON A TOPOGRAPHIC MAP?

Topographic maps can't show every detail about a place. Cartographers must focus on the purpose of the map when deciding what to show.

Topographic maps often include only a few human-made features. They focus mostly on showing elevations.

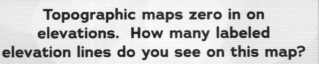

Topographic maps zero in on elevations. How many labeled elevation lines do you see on this map?

Topographic maps look unlike any other maps because of their rings of lines. A single contour line on a topographic map is known as an isoline. An isoline is a line that has a single value, or measurement. A contour line is an isoline because it marks a single elevation.

This map of Mount Everest shows many isolines.

Scales

Topographic maps might be different from other maps, but they do have several typical map features. They often have a scale. Places on maps can't be drawn at their actual size. The cartographer would run out of paper! Instead, cartographers draw places smaller than they actually are. Then cartographers include a scale on the map explaining that a certain distance on the map stands for a certain distance on Earth.

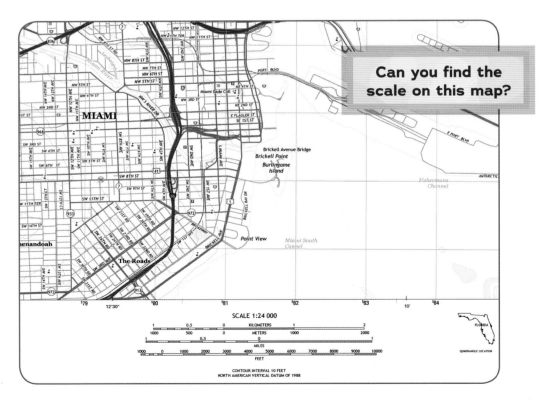

Can you find the scale on this map?

The Contour Interval

Topographic maps use a scale to tell you distance. They also tell you the vertical distance between contour lines, called the contour interval. The contour interval is usually stated under the scale. For example, a topographic map might note that its contour lines are at intervals of 40 feet (12 m). On that map, you would find a contour line where the land raises or lowers by 40 feet.

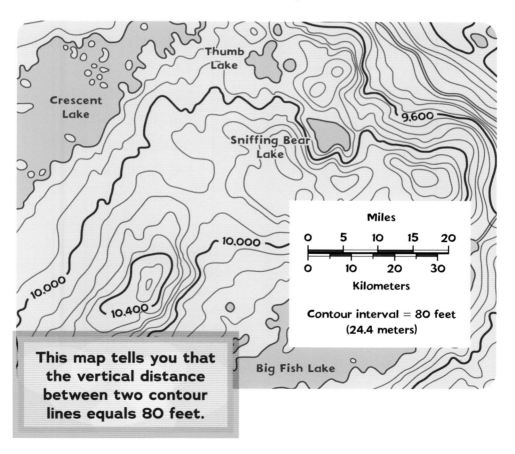

Thumb Lake

Crescent Lake

9,600

Sniffing Bear Lake

10,000

Miles

| 0 | 5 | 10 | 15 | 20 |

| 0 | 10 | 20 | 30 |

Kilometers

Contour interval = 80 feet
(24.4 meters)

10,000

10,000

10,400

Big Fish Lake

This map tells you that the vertical distance between two contour lines equals 80 feet.

Legends

Topographic maps also often have legends, or keys. Legends explain what the different symbols or colors on a map mean. They might show that a dot stands for a city or that blue stands for a lake.

On topographic maps, the legend is another place where you might find the difference in elevation between two contour lines. If this isn't explained under the scale, it will often be explained in the legend.

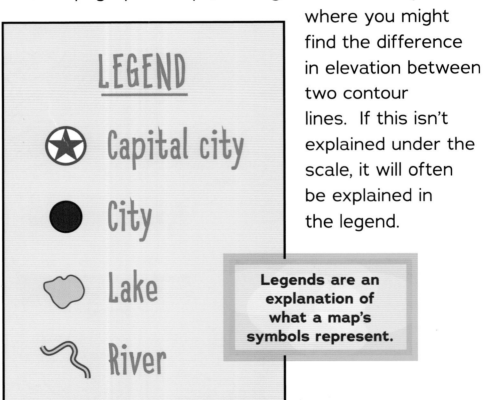

Legends are an explanation of what a map's symbols represent.

Helpful Colors

Topographic maps use colors to add bonus information for readers. The USGS uses the colors below in its topographic maps:

- Brown for contour lines
- Blue for water features
- Green for plants, such as forests or plains
- Red for major roads
- Black for minor roads, buildings, and other human-made features
- Purple for changes from an existing map
- White for glaciers or flat, empty lands

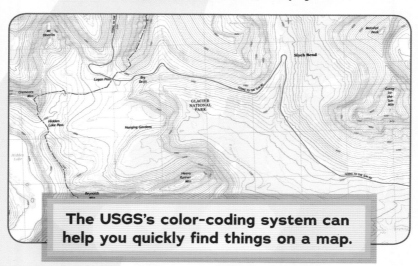

The USGS's color-coding system can help you quickly find things on a map.

The Compass Rose

Another thing you might find on a topographic map is a compass rose. A compass rose shows direction. It lets you know which way is north, east, south, and west on a map. Many compass roses are labeled with the first letter of each of the four directions. Some are labeled only with an *N* for north.

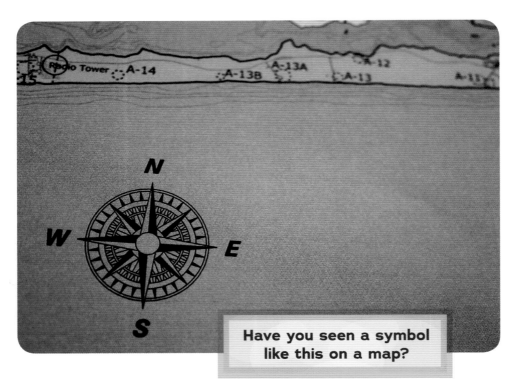

Have you seen a symbol like this on a map?

Latitude and Longitude Lines

Topographic maps often have vertical and horizontal lines running across them. These lines are different from contour lines. They are called latitude and longitude lines. Latitude lines show north and south positions. Longitude lines show east and west positions.

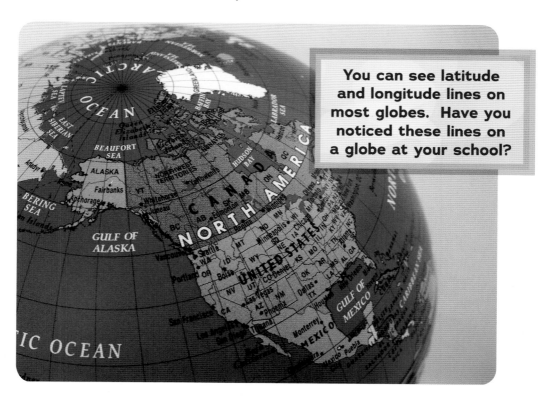

You can see latitude and longitude lines on most globes. Have you noticed these lines on a globe at your school?

The Equator

You may also see a thick latitude line running right across the middle of a map. This is the equator. It is not an actual line that exists on Earth. If you travel to where it is on the map, you won't see a line on the ground. It exists only on maps. The equator tells you where the midpoint is between the North Pole and South Pole.

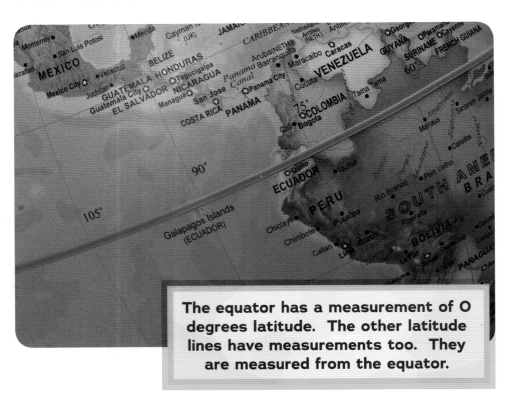

The equator has a measurement of 0 degrees latitude. The other latitude lines have measurements too. They are measured from the equator.

The Prime Meridian

Some topographic maps are labeled with the prime meridian. The prime meridian is a longitude line. Like the equator, it doesn't exist on Earth. It is the main vertical line around a globe from the North Pole to South Pole. It runs through Greenwich, England.

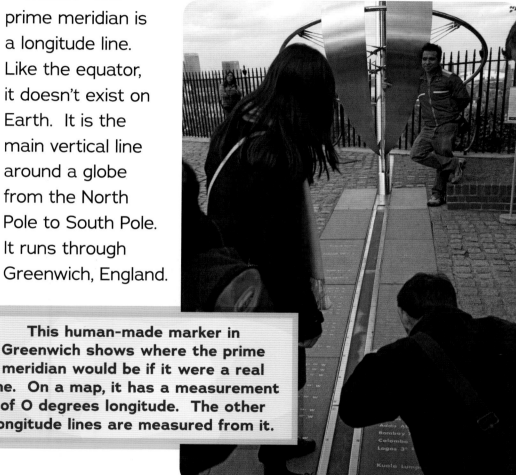

This human-made marker in Greenwich shows where the prime meridian would be if it were a real line. On a map, it has a measurement of 0 degrees longitude. The other longitude lines are measured from it.

Maps of All Kinds

Topographic maps today may be printed on paper or displayed digitally. On a computer, a geographic information system (GIS) links maps and digital data. It layers visual information such as land and water features over certain positions on Earth's surface. One map can show a lot of data about one place.

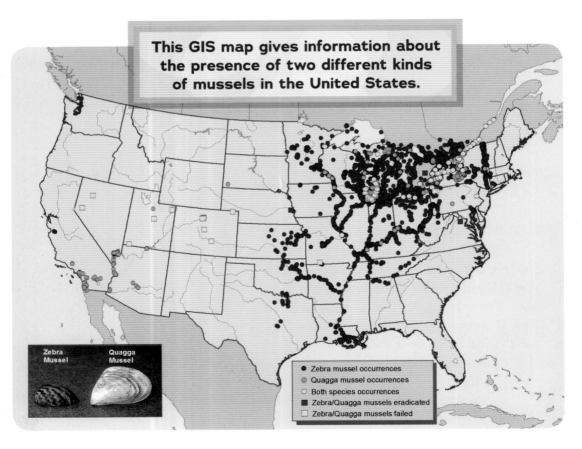

This GIS map gives information about the presence of two different kinds of mussels in the United States.

Zebra Mussel   Quagga Mussel

- ● Zebra mussel occurrences
- ● Quagga mussel occurrences
- ○ Both species occurrences
- ■ Zebra/Quagga mussels eradicated
- □ Zebra/Quagga mussels failed

GIS topographic maps can layer weather forecasts and details about a specific event, such as an oil spill, over one location. This can give aid workers at an oil spill site valuable information they can use in cleanup efforts. It can guide them to the worst part of the spill or tell them if a storm is coming. Past and current maps can be layered too. This allows scientists to look for patterns and connections that might affect people in the future.

GIS TOPOGRAPHIC MAPS HELP AID WORKERS DO THEIR JOBS.

Did You Know?

The National Oceanic and Atmospheric Administration (NOAA) uses topographic maps and GIS to create maps that forecast floods. This helps people know when to leave an area for a safer place when a flood is expected. It can also help people take precautions to lessen flood damage to their homes. Topographic maps and GIS can help save lives and property.

Sandbags such as these can help keep floodwaters out of a home.

Chapter 3

HOW DO YOU USE A TOPOGRAPHIC MAP?

Topographic maps guide people who enjoy the outdoors. Think of hikers, campers, cross-country skiers, hunters, mountain climbers, bicyclists, and off-road drivers. They like to know the terrain (physical land features) for their activities.

Topographic maps can help you have fun! How might they help those who enjoy outdoor activities?

Topographic maps show terrain that could be dangerous, such as cliffs, caves, waterfalls, or swamps. The Grand Canyon National Park features a gorge 1 mile (1.6 kilometers) deep that runs 277 miles (446 km) through worn rock. Maps are important for backcountry visitors. Without knowing about gorges like this one, the visitors could get hurt.

Maps can help keep people safe when they are visiting an unfamiliar area.

Topographic maps gauge distances from place to place. This helps people plan safe routes to match the outdoor activity. Can you hike as easily on steep mountain trails as you can on flat meadow paths?

It's a good idea to plan your route before setting out on an adventure.

Topographic maps show human-made features that relate to the map's purpose. A hiking map may include bridges, rest areas, or paved roads that might come in handy on an adventure. A topographic map for planning and building a new road would look very different.

Topographic hiking maps can be useful to hikers, bikers, and others interested in exploring natural areas.

Helping Scientists

Topographic maps help scientists understand land features and changes to them that impact the environment. The maps can alert scientists to places at risk from a hurricane. They can point out spots on Earth where an earthquake might be likely to occur.

Changes to the landscape in New Orleans (ABOVE) can affect the damage from hurricanes there.

Helping Firefighters

Firefighters use topographic maps to battle wildfires. Fires move uphill faster as the land gets steeper. Flames can reach fuel, such as dry grass, more easily on hills.

Heat rises and dries out plants uphill, making the fire spread more quickly on slopes than on flat ground.

Topographic maps help firefighters keep wildfires like this one from spreading.

Did You Know?

If forest fires wipe out trees on hilly terrain, the terrain may weaken. Then rain could wash soil downhill, causing mudslides. Topographic maps show areas at risk of experiencing mudslides. This is yet another way topographic maps help keep people safe.

Areas without trees are especially likely to experience mudslides.

Helping Farmers

Farmers use topographic maps to plan their land use. Flat fields may work well for planting crops. Hilly land that creates small ponds may be better for cattle.

Topographic maps can identify spots that are ideal for raising cattle.

Farmers may want to drill underground for water to grow crops. A topographic map can suggest where to tap an aquifer (a layer of rock or sand that can absorb and hold water). The USGS tracks the High Plains aquifer, one of the largest in the world. The aquifer measures about 174,000 square miles (450,658 sq. km) beneath parts of South Dakota, Nebraska, Wyoming, Colorado, Kansas, Oklahoma, New Mexico, and Texas. USGS topographic maps show the water's flow. Comparing maps over time also reveals how this important resource is changing.

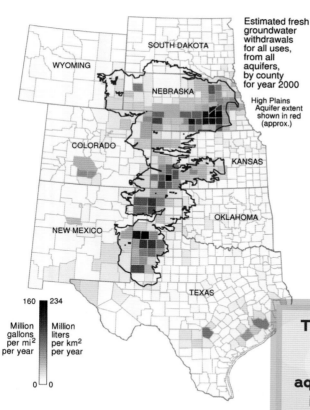

Estimated fresh groundwater withdrawals for all uses, from all aquifers, by county for year 2000

High Plains Aquifer extent shown in red (approx.)

160 ▮ 234

Million gallons per mi^2 per year | Million liters per km^2 per year

0 ▭ 0

SOUTH DAKOTA
WYOMING
NEBRASKA
COLORADO
KANSAS
OKLAHOMA
NEW MEXICO
TEXAS

The red line on this map shows the area from which the High Plains aquifer drew groundwater in one particular year.

Helping Sailors

Ship captains and boaters use topographic maps of rivers, lakes, and oceans. These maps guide them away from dangerous rocks and show safe harbors. Fishers use the maps to find schools of fish that swim in certain depths.

Pinpointing spots where certain fish swim is essential to people who fish for a living.

Chapter 4

ARE YOU A TOPOGRAPHIC MAP WHIZ?

Now that you've learned about topographic maps, it's time to put your knowledge to the test. But don't worry. You won't be graded on this test. You'll even get to have some fun. You'll be taking an imaginary trip to the Appalachian National Scenic Trail!

This map shows the Appalachian National Scenic Trail. What states does it run through?

To start your adventure, pretend you've been invited to join a hike for a day on the trail. The Appalachian National Scenic Trail is the longest footpath in the world. You couldn't possibly hike the whole thing in one day! So your group is going to hike on the trail through New Hampshire, as shown on the map below. What is the elevation at Mount Washington? What other mountains will you see?

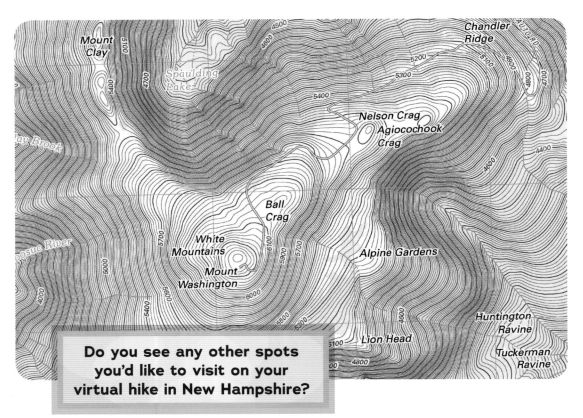

Do you see any other spots you'd like to visit on your virtual hike in New Hampshire?

The Appalachian Trail winds through mostly wild areas. Why would people choose to hike in the wilderness far from other people? What are some reasons to choose to hike near a city?

You can go on walking adventures in the city if you can't make it to the wilderness.

You Did It!

Awesome job! You've just used a topographic map. These maps help you explore and learn more about your world. What would you like to learn from a topographic map?

YOU CAN LEARN A LOT BY STUDYING MAPS AND GLOBES!

Fun Facts

- In 2009, the USGS began creating what it calls topo maps. These maps are based on traditional maps that the USGS made between 1947 and 1992, but they have been updated using GIS data.

- The USGS used more than six hundred million measurements taken by space vehicles to produce topographic maps of Mars.

- Some geography fans go on hunts for spots where longitude and latitude lines meet. These spots are called confluence points. The geography buffs use GPS to find these points. They keep track of them as part of the Degree Confluence Project.

Glossary

aerial: taken or seen from a spot above Earth. Aerial photography is taken from above Earth, usually from an airplane.

cartographer: a person who makes maps

compass rose: a circle showing directions on a map

contour line: a line that shows elevation

elevation: the height of a place or a thing

equator: an imaginary circle around Earth halfway between the North Pole and the South Pole

gorge: a narrow passage through land

isoline: a line that has a single value, or measurement

latitude: a distance north or south of the equator measured in degrees

legend: an explanatory list of symbols on a map

longitude: a distance east or west measured in degrees of the prime meridian

prime meridian: the 0-degree longitude that runs through Greenwich, England

scale: a tool that explains the size of a map compared to the actual place it represents

LERNER

SOURCE™

Expand learning beyond the printed book. Download free, complementary educational resources for this book from our website, www.lernerresource.com.

Learn More about Topographic Maps

Books

Higgins, Nadia. *US Geography through Infographics*. Minneapolis: Lerner Publications, 2015. Geography buffs will love this fun, highly visual take on geography in the United States.

Hirsch, Rebecca E. *Using Physical Maps*. Minneapolis: Lerner Publications, 2017. In this interesting book, readers will learn about maps that show physical landscape features.

Panchyk, Richard. *Charting the World: Geography and Maps from Cave Paintings to GPS*. Chicago: Chicago Review Press, 2011. Find out more about mapmaking in the past and present.

Websites

Enchanted Learning: World Geography
http://www.enchantedlearning.com/geography
Check out this collection of maps, printouts, flags, and more from Enchanted Learning.

50 States
http://www.50states.com
This site has fun facts about the fifty states and many maps that you can print.

National Geographic Kids Atlases
http://www.nationalgeographic.com/kids-world-atlas/maps.html
Create your own maps, find reference maps, and learn about different cultures at this site.

Index

Photo Acknowledgments

The images in this book are used with the permission of: US Geological Survey, pp. 4, 12, 15, 20, 31, 34; © EdgeofReason/Dreamstime.com, p. 5; © Greg Dale/National Geographic Creative, p. 6; Map by William Hole and John Smith, courtesy of Library of Congress, p. 7; © Gaetan Bally/Keystone/Corbis, p. 8; © iStockphoto.com/Geostorm, p. 9; © Pixelrobot/Dreamstime.com, p. 10; © Barker Vail/Small World Maps LLC, p. 11; © Laura Westlund/Independent Picture Service, pp. 13, 14; © Kevin Zimarik/Dreamstime.com, p. 16; © duncan1890/Getty Images, p. 17; © iStockphoto.com/Juanmonino, p. 18; © geogphotos/Alamy, p. 19; © David McNew/Stringer/Getty Images, p. 21; © Monkey Business Images/Shutterstock.com, p. 22; © iStockphoto.com/mbbirdy, p. 23; © robin.runck.de/Deposit Photos, p. 24; © iStockphoto.com/omgimages, p. 25; © iStockphoto.com/stockstudioX, p. 26; © Melanie Stetson Freeman/Christian Science Monitor/Getty Images, p. 27; © iStockphoto.com/EdStock, p. 28; © Al Seib/Los Angeles Times/Getty Images, p. 29; © yuriyzhuravov/Deposit Photos, p. 30; © iStockphoto.com/Steve Froebe, p. 32; © Appalachian Trail Conservancy, p. 33; © iStockphoto.com/Rich Legg, p. 35; © iStockphoto.com/Christopher Futcher, p. 36.

Front cover: © Laura Westlund/Independent Picture Service (USA map); US Geological Survey (Grand Canyon map); © iStockphoto.com/mrgao (magnifying glass); © iStockphoto.com/Devaev Dmitriy (background).

Main body text set in Adrianna Regular 14/20.
Typeface provided by Chank.